Mozart Arias

Edited by
Robert L. Larsen and Richard Walters

To access companion recorded accompaniments online, visit:
www.halleonard.com/mylibrary
Enter Code
3725-1998-9685-1415

Aria Text Editor and Translator: Martha Gerhart
Assistant Editor: Janet Neis

On the cover, Nicolas Lancret, *La Camargo Dancing*, c. 1730, oil on canvas, 30 x 42 inches,
Andrew W. Mellon Collection, © 1992 National Gallery of Art, Washington

ISBN: 978-0-7935-6239-8

7777 W. BLUEMOUND RD. P.O. BOX 13819 MILWAUKEE, WI 53213

Visit Hal Leonard Online at
www.halleonard.com

ROBERT L. LARSEN is the compiler and editor of the bestselling *G. Schirmer Opera Anthology,* in five volumes, and also collaborated with Evelyn Lear in recorded and published master classes, released by G. Schirmer in two volumes, *Lyric Soprano Arias: A Master Class with Evelyn Lear.* Dr. Larsen is featured as a pianist on a CD/score package of *Songs of Joseph Marx* from Hal Leonard Publishing, and is compiler of a series of opera scenes for study and workshop performances.

Dr. Larsen is founder and artistic director of one of America's major opera festivals, the critically acclaimed Des Moines Metro Opera, and since the company's founding in 1973 has served as conductor and stage director for all of its productions. Since 1965 Dr. Larsen has also been chairman of the department of music at Simpson College in Indianola, Iowa, and during his tenure the department has received national recognition and awards for its serious and extensive program of operatic training for undergraduates. He holds a bachelor's degree from Simpson College, a master's degree in piano performance from the University of Michigan, and a doctorate in opera and conducting from Indiana University. His piano studies were with Sven Lekberg, Joseph Brinkman, Rudolph Ganz, and Walter Bricht. Dr. Larsen is highly regarded as an opera coach and accompanist. He has coached singers at Tanglewood, Oglebay Park, West Virginia, Chicago, and New York, and has assisted in the training of many artists with significant operatic careers.

Dr. Larsen was the recipient of the first Governor's Award in Music presented by the Iowa Arts Council, and is listed in "Who's Who in America." In addition to his many other musical accomplishments, he is an avid student of the Renaissance, and specializes in bringing to life the great vocal works of that period.

Contents

MOZART ARIAS FOR SOPRANO

LUCIO SILLA

The libretto is by Giovanni da Gamerra, with alterations by Pietro Metastasio. The opera was premiered at the Teatro Regio Ducale in Milan on December 26, 1772. The story is set in ancient Rome.

Pupille amate

from Act III
character: Cecilio

Cecilio has returned from exile to see his fiancée Giunia, whom the dictator Lucio Silla also wants to marry. When Silla proclaims publicly that Giunia will be his bride, Giunia threatens to stab herself. Cecilio rushes to her defense and is condemned to death. Giunia vows to die with Cecilio rather than marry Silla. Cecilio tells her that her tears and suffering are worse to him than death. (Cecilio may also be sung by a mezzo-soprano.)

Pupille amate,	*Beloved eyes,*
non lagrimate,	*do not weep;*
morir mi fate	*you make me perish*
pria di morir.	*before dying.*
Quest'alma fida	*This faithful soul,*
a voi d'intorno	*encircling you,*
farà ritorno,	*will return,*
sciolta in sospir.	*liberated in sighs.*

IDOMENEO
(Re di Creta)
(Idomeneo, King of Crete)

The libretto is by Abbé Giambattista Varesco, after the libretto *Idomenée* by Antoine Danchet (set to music by Antoine Campra and premiered in Paris in 1712). The story is based on ancient legend. The opera was premiered at the Hoftheater in Munich on January 29, 1781. The setting is the Port of Sidon on the island of Crete, shortly before the end of the Trojan war, about 1200 B.C.

Zeffiretti lusinghieri

from Act III
character: Ilia

In an attempt to hide his son Idamante from the gods, Idomeneo sends him on a journey to Argos. Idamante's beloved, Ilia, contemplates his departure.

Zeffiretti lusinghieri,	*Charming breezes,*
deh volate al mio tesoro,	*pray, fly to my dear one,*
e gli dite, ch'io l'adoro,	*and tell him that I adore him;*
che mi serbi il cor fedel.	*may he preserve his faithful heart for me.*
E voi piante, e fior sinceri,	*And you, plants and truthful flowers,*
che ora inaffia il pianto amaro,	*which my bitter tears now moisten,*
dite a lui, che amor più raro	*tell him that love more rare*
mai vedeste sotto al ciel.	*you have never seen beneath heaven.*

DIE ENTFÜHRUNG AUS DEM SERAIL
(The Abduction from the Seraglio)

The libretto is by Gottlieb Stephanie the Younger, adapted from *Belmont und Constanze* by Christoph Friedrich Bretzner (set to music by Johann André and premiered in Berlin in 1781). The opera was premiered at the Burgtheater in Vienna on July 16, 1782. The story is set at the country palace of the Pasha Selim in Turkey during the sixteenth century.

Welche Wonne, welche Lust

from Act II
character: Blonde

Constanze, her maid Blonde, and Blonde's sweetheart Pedrillo have been captured by Turkish pirates and are now held at the palace of the Pasha Selim. Belmonte, Constanze's beloved, at long last has found the palace and has told Pedrillo of his plans to rescue the party. When Blonde hears of the plans from Pedrillo, she is overjoyed and can hardly wait to tell Constanze the news.

Welche Wonne, welche Lust	*What rapture, what joy*
regt sich nun in meiner Brust!	*stirs now in my breast!*
Voller Freuden will ich springen,	*Full of delight I will run*
ihr die frohe Nachricht bringen,	*to bring her the happy news*
und mit Lachen und mit Scherzen	*and, with laughter and with fun,*
ihrem schwachen, kranken Herzen	*to her faint, ailing heart*
Trost und Rettung prophezeih'n.	*prophesy comfort and deliverance.*

LE NOZZE DI FIGARO
(The Marriage of Figaro)

The libretto is by Lorenzo da Ponte, based on the comedy *La Folle Journée, ou Le Mariage de Figaro* by Pierre-Auguste Caron de Beaumarchais. The play was premiered in Paris in 1784; the opera was premiered at the Burgtheater in Vienna on May 1, 1786. The story is set at the palace of Count Almaviva, near Seville, in the seventeenth century (usually played as the eighteenth century).

Porgi, amor

from Act II
character: Countess

Countess Almaviva, still young and beautiful, knows that her husband has developed a roving eye for other ladies of the castle, and is shamed and hurt by his neglect and deceit. Alone in her bed chamber as the act opens, she prays to the god of love to assist her in her hour of need.

Porgi, amor, qualche ristoro	*Grant, Love, some relief*
al mio duolo, a' miei sospir!	*to my sorrow, to my sighing!*
O mi rendi il mio tesoro,	*Either give me back my beloved,*
o mi lascia almen morir!	*or just let me die!*

Deh vieni, non tardar

from Act IV
character: Susanna

The Countess is disguised as her chamber maid, Susanna, in order to trick her husband, the Count, who thinks he is meeting Susanna herself. Susanna, married only hours before to Figaro, appears disguised as her mistress and sings this recitative and arietta, which seems to be the girl's enchanting imitation of the Countess' restrained and elegant way of speaking and singing. Susanna is aware that her husband is listening.

Giunse alfin il momento	*The moment has finally arrived*
che godrò senza affanno	*which I will enjoy, without anxiety,*
in braccio all'idol mio.	*in the arms of my idol.*
Timide cure! uscite dal mio petto;	*Timid feelings, leave my breast;*
a turbar non venite il mio diletto!	*don't come to disturb my pleasure!*
Oh come par che all'amoroso foco	*Oh, how it seems that to amorous passion*
l'amenità del loco,	*the pleasantness of the place,*
la terra e il ciel risponda,	*the earth, and the sky respond,*
come la notte i furti miei seconda!	*as the darkness favors my connivings!*
Deh vieni,	*Please come;*
non tardar, o gioja bella.	*don't delay, oh beautiful joy.*
Vieni ove amore per goder t'appella	*Come to where love calls you to enjoy yourself*
finchè non splende in ciel	*until the nocturnal torch doesn't*
notturna face—	*shine in the sky anymore--*
Finchè l'aria è ancor bruna,	*until it's dark again,*
e il mondo tace.	*and the world is still.*
Qui mormora il ruscel,	*Here murmurs the stream;*
qui scherza l'aura,	*here plays the breeze*
che col dolce susurro	*which, with its gentle rustling,*
il cor ristaura,	*revives the heart.*
qui ridono i fioretti	*Here little flowers are laughing,*
e l'erba è fresca.	*and the grass is fresh.*
Ai piaceri d'amor	*To the pleasures of love*
qui tutto adesca.	*everything here is enticing.*
Vieni, ben mio,	*Come, my dear,*
tra queste piante ascose!	*among these sheltering trees!*
Ti vo' la fronte incoronar di rose.	*I want to crown your head with roses.*

DON GIOVANNI

The libretto is by Lorenzo da Ponte, after Giovanni Bertati's libretto for Giuseppe Gazzaniga's opera *Il convitato di pietra;* also after the Don Juan legends. Don Giovanni was premiered at the National Theater in Prague on October 29, 1787. The story is set in and near Seville during the seventeenth century (usually played as the eighteenth century).

Batti, batti, o bel Masetto

from Act I
character: Zerlina

Zerlina and Masetto, a peasant couple, are about to be married. The festivities have begun when Giovanni happens on the scene and becomes enamored of the charming Zerlina. He tries to lead her to his castle and almost succeeds. Following the near seduction, Zerlina teases and kisses her offended fiancé into good humor again.

Ma se colpa io non ho!	*But I'm not guilty!*
Ma se da lui ingannata rismasi…	*But I was tricked by him…*
E poi che temi?	*And so what are you afraid of?*
Tranquillati, mia vita:	*Be assured, love of my life:*
non mi toccò la punta delle dita.	*he didn't touch the tip of my finger.*
Non me lo credi? Ingrato!	*Don't you believe me? Ungrateful!*
Vien qui, sfogati, ammazzami—	*Come here; vent your anger; kill me—*
fa' tutto di me quel che ti piace;	*do anything you please to me.*
ma poi, Masetto mio, fa' pace.	*But afterwards, my Masetto, make peace.*

Batti, o bel Masetto,	*Hit, oh handsome Masetto,*
la tua povera Zerlina.	*your poor Zerlina.*
Starò qui come agnellina	*Like a little lamb*
le tue botte ad aspettar.	*I'll await your blows.*
Lascerò straziarmi il crine,	*I'll let my hair be pulled out.*
lascerò cavarmi gli occhi,	*I'll let my eyes be scratched out.*
e le care tue manine lieta poi	*And then, happy, I will be able to kiss*
saprò baciar.	*your dear beloved hands.*
Ah, lo vedo, non hai core:	*Ah, I see it: you don't have courage!*
Pace, o vita mia;	*Peace, oh love of my life;*
in contenti ed allegria	*in contentment and good cheer*
notte e dì vogliam passar, sì…	*let's enjoy passing the nights and days—yes…*

Vedrai, carino

from Act II
character: Zerlina

Don Giovanni, disguised as his servant Leporello, viciously beats the peasant lad Masetto. When Zerlina, the boy's bride-to-be comes on the scene, she sympathizes with Masetto, assuring him that she can heal all his wounds.

Vedrai, carino, se sei buonino,	*You will see, dearest, if you are good,*
che bel rimedio ti voglio dar.	*what fine medicine I want to give you.*
È naturale, non da disgusto,	*It's natural; it's not unpleasant;*
e lo speziale non lo sa far,	*and the pharmacist doesn't know how to make it—*
no, non lo sa far.	*no, he doesn't know how to make it.*
È un certo balsamo che porto addosso.	*It's a certain balm that I carry with me.*
Dare te'l posso, se'l vuoi provar.	*I can give it to you, if you want to try it.*
Saper vorresti dove mi sta?	*Would you like to know where I have it?*
Sentilo battere, toccami qua.	*Feel it beat; touch me here.*

COSÌ FAN TUTTE
(Women Are Like That)

The libretto is an original story by Lorenzo da Ponte. The opera was premiered at the Burgtheater in Vienna on January 26, 1790. The story is set at the home of Fiordiligi and her sister, Dorabella, in Naples during the seventeenth century (most often played as the eighteenth century).

Una donna a quindici anni

from Act II
character: Despina

Don Alfonso has a plan to prove to his young friends Ferrando and Guglielmo that their girlfriends, Fiordiligi and Dorabella, can be tempted into faithlessness. Ferrando and Guglielmo, eager to prove the ladies' fidelity, have disguised themselves as wealthy Albanians and have courted the sisters. As Act II opens, the maid Despina chides the two ladies for their faithfulness to absent lovers, suggesting that they follow her example.

Una donna a quindici anni	*A girl at age fifteen*
dee saper ogni gran moda,	*ought to know all worldly ways:*
dove il diavolo ha la coda,	*all sorts of deceptions,* *
cosa è bene, e mal cos'è;	*what is good, and what is bad;*
dee saper le maliziette,	*she ought to know the little tricks*
che innamorano gli amanti,	*that charm lovers:*
finger riso, finger pianti,	*to feign laughter, to feign tears,*
inventar i bei perchè.	*to invent good excuses.*
Dee in un momento dar retta a cento,	*She must pay attention to a hundred men at once,*
colle pupille parlar con mille,	*talk to a thousand with her eyes,*
dar speme a tutti, sien belli o brutti,	*give hope to all, be they handsome or ugly,*
saper nascondersi senza confondersi,	*know how to be secretive without getting flustered,*
senza arrosire saper mentire,	*without blushing, know how to lie,*
e qual regina dall'alto soglio	*and, like a queen from her lofty throne,*
col «posso e voglio» farsi ubbidir.	*with "I can" and "I want," be obeyed.*
Par ch'abbian gusto	*It seems that they're taking a liking*
di tal dottrina;	*to such a doctrine;*
viva Despina,	*long live Despina,*
che sa servir.	*who knows how to be of service!*

*An idiomatic expression; literal translation of the words is "where the devil has his tail."

LA CLEMENZA DI TITO
(The Clemency of Titus)

The libretto is by Caterino Mazzolà, adapted from a libretto by Pietro Metastasio (set to music by Antonio Caldara and first performed in Vienna in 1734). *La Clemenza di Tito* was premiered at the National Theater in Prague on September 6, 1791. The story is set in Rome, c. 80 A.D.

S'altro che lagrime

from Act II
character: Servilia

Vitellia seduced Sesto, and then convinced him to destroy his friend, the Emperor Tito. Sesto has been sentenced to death for killing a man he mistook for Tito. When Vitellia refuses to confess her own guilt to Tito, Sesto's sister Servilia tells her that she is cruel to offer her tears for Sesto but not her help.

S'altro che lagrime per lui non tenti,	*If you don't attempt something other than tears for him,*
tutto il tuo piangere non gioverà.	*all your weeping will be in vain.*
A quest'inutile pietà che senti,	*To this useless pity which you feel,*
oh quanto è simile la crudeltà.	*oh, how similar is cruelty.*

DIE ZAUBERFLÖTE
(The Magic Flute)

The libretto is by Emanuel Schikaneder, based on a fairy tale from the collection *Dschinnistan* by Christoph Martin Wieland (three volumes, published in Weimar beginning in 1786). The *Singspiel* was premiered at the Theater auf der Wieden in Vienna on September 30, 1791. The story is set in legendary, ancient Egypt.

Ach, ich fühl's

from Act II
character: Pamina

Pamina is despondent because her beloved, the Prince Tamino, no longer speaks to her and seems to shun her presence. She does not know that he has sworn a vow of silence as part of the ceremony of initiation to Sarastro's brotherhood.

Ach, ich fühl's, es ist verschwunden,	*Ah, I feel it; it has vanished—*
ewig hin der Liebe Glück!	*forever gone, the happiness of love!*
Nimmer kommt ihr, Wonnestunden,	*Never will you, blissful hours, come*
meinem Herzen mehr zurück.	*back again to my heart.*
Sieh, Tamino, diese Tränen fließen,	*See, Tamino, these tears flow,*
Trauter, dir allein.	*beloved one, for you alone.*
Fühlst du nicht der Liebe Sehnen,	*If you do not feel the longing of love,*
so wird Ruh im Tode sein.	*then peace will come to be in death.*

Pupille amate

from
LUCIO SILLA

Tempo di menuetto

CECILIO:

fa - te pri - a di___ mo - rir,_____ mo - rir___ mi fa - te

pri - a di___ mo - rir, mo - rir___ mi fa - te_____

pri - a di mo - rir.

Quest' al - ma___ fi - da

mo - rir mi fa - te pria di mo - rir. Pu - pil - le a-

ma - te, non la - gri - ma - te,

mo - rir___ mi___ fa - te pri - a di___ mo - rir,_____

mo - rir___ mi___ fa - te pri - a di mo - rir. Pu - pil - le a

15

ma - te, non la-gri-ma - te, mo-rir mi fa - te

pria di mo - rir, _____ mo-rir mi fa - te pria di mo - rir,

mo - rir_ mi_ fa - te pri-a_ di mo - rir.

Zeffiretti lusinghieri

from
IDOMENEO

Zef - fi - ret - ti lu - sin - ghie - ri, deh vo—

la - te al mio te - so - ro, e gli di - te, ch'io l'a - do - ro,

che mi ser - bi il cor____ fe - del, che mi

ser - bi il cor____ fe - del,_____ il

ro, di - te a lui,___ che a mor___ più ra - ro

mai ___ ve - de - ste___ sot - to al ciel, sot - to al ciel.___ Zef - fi -

ret - ti lu - sin - ghie - ri, deh vo - la - - -

- - - - - -

te al mio te - so - ro, e gli di - te, ch'io l'a-

do - ro, che mi serbi il cor___ fe - del. Zef - fi-

ret - ti lu - sin - ghie - ri, deh vo - la - te al mio te - so - ro, e gli

di - te, ch'io l'a - do - ro, che mi ser - bi il cor___ fe-

del, che mi ser - bi il cor____ fe - del,____

il cor____ fe - del,____

il cor____ fe - del.

mfp

p

mfp

mfp

p

Welche Wonne, welche Lust

from
DIE ENTFÜHRUNG AUS DEM SERAIL

Brust! Vol - ler Freu - den will ich sprin - gen,

ihr die fro - he Nach - richt brin - gen, und mit La - chen und mit

Scher - zen ih - rem schwa - chen,_ kran - ken Her - zen Trost und_

Ret - tung pro - phe - zeih'n, Trost und Ret - tung pro - phe - zeih'n.

Vol - ler Freu-den will ich sprin-gen,

ihr die fro - he Nach-richt brin-gen, und mit La - chen und mit Scher-zen ih - rem

schwa-chen, kran-ken Her-zen, ih - rem schwa - chen, schwa - chen, kran - ken

Her - - - zen Trost und Ret - tung pro - phe -

zeih'n,___ Trost und Ret - tung__ pro - phe - zeih'n, Trost und

Ret - tung pro - phe - zeih'n,___ pro - phe - zeih'n. Wel-che Won - ne, wel - che

Lust regt sich nun in mei - ner Brust, wel - che Won - ne, wel - che

Lust regt sich nun in mei - ner Brust!

Vol - ler Freu - den will ich sprin - gen,

ihr die fro - he Nach - richt brin - gen, und mit La - chen und mit

Scher - zen ih - rem schwa - chen, kran - ken Her - zen Trost und

Ret - tung pro - phe - zeih'n, Trost und Ret - tung pro - phe - zeih'n. Vol - ler

fp   cresc.   f   f

Freu-den will ich sprin-gen, ihr die fro-he Nach-richt

brin-gen, und mit La-chen und mit Scher-zen ih-rem schwa-chen, kran-ken Her-zen, ih-rem

schwa-chen,__ schwa-chen,__ kran-ken__ Her - zen

Trost und Ret - tung pro - phe - zeih'n,__ Trost und Ret - tung__

Won - ne, wel - che Lust regt sich nun in mei - ner Brust, wel - che

Won - ne, wel - che Lust regt sich nun in mei - ner

Brust,_____ in mei - ner Brust,_____ in mei - ner

Brust!

Porgi, amor

from
LE NOZZE DI FIGARO

CONTESSA:

Por - gi,a - mor,— qual - che ri -

sto - ro al mio duo - lo, a' mie - i so -

spir! — O mi —

ren - di il mio te - so - ro, O mi —

la - scia al-men mo - rir, o mi la - scia al-men mo - rir! Por-gi, a-mor, qual-che ri -

cresc.

f   *p*

sto - ro al mio duo-lo, a' miei so - spir! O mi ren - di il mio te -

so - ro, o mi la - - - scia al - men mo - rir, al -

men mo - rir, o mi ren - di il mio te - so - ro, o mi

la - scia al - men mo - rir!

*Appoggiatura optional

Deh vieni, non tardar

from
LE NOZZE DI FIGARO

*Appoggiatura recommended

sci - te dal mio pet - to;   a tur - bar   non ve - ni - te il mio di - let - to!

Oh co - me par che all' a - mo - ro - so

fo - co l'a - me - ni - tà del lo - co, la ter - ra e il ciel ri - spon - da,

co - me la not - te i fur - ti miei se - con - da!

[Andante]

p

Deh vie - ni, non tar - dar, o gio - ja bel - la.

Vie-ni o-ve a-mo - re per go-der t'ap-pel - la fin - chè non splen-de in

ciel not-tur-na fa-ce— fin - chè l'a-ria e an-cor bru-na, e il mon - do

ta - ce.   Qui mor - mo-ra il ru -

scel,__ qui scher - za l'au - ra,   che col dol-ce su - sur-ro il cor ri -

stau - ra,   qui ri - do-no i fio - ret-ti e l'er-ba è fre - sca.

Ai pia - ce-ri d'a - mor qui tut-to a - de - sca.   Vie - ni, ben

mi - o, tra___ que - ste pian - te a - sco - se, vie - ni,

vie - ni! Ti vo' la fron - te in - co - ro - nar___ di ro -

colla voce

se, ti vo' la fron - te in - co - ro - nar,___ in - co - ro -

nar___ di ro - se.

colla voce

Batti, batti, o bel Masetto

from
DON GIOVANNI

ZERLINA:

secco recitativo

Ma se col-pa_io non ho! Ma se da lui in-gan-na - ta ri - ma - si... E poi che te - mi? Tran - quil - la - ti, mia vi - ta: non mi toc - cò la pun-ta del-le di - ta. Non me lo cre - di? In - gra - to! Vien qui, sfo - ga - ti, am - maz - za - mi— fa' tut - to di me quel che ti pia - ce; ma poi, Ma-set - to mi - o, ma poi fa' pa - ce.

*Appoggiatura recommended

attacca l'aria

Vedrai, carino

from
DON GIOVANNI

non lo sa far, no, non lo sa far._____ È un cer - to bal - sa - mo

che por-to ad-dos - so. Da-re tel pos - so, se il vuoi pro - var._____

Sa - per vor - re - sti do - ve mi

sta, do-ve, do-ve, do-ve mi sta?_____

Sen - ti - lo— bat - te - re,— toc - ca - mi qua, qua, toc - ca - mi

qua, qua, toc - ca - mi qua,— qua, toc - ca - mi qua.

cresc.

f

p

pp

Una donna a quindici anni

from
COSÌ FAN TUTTE

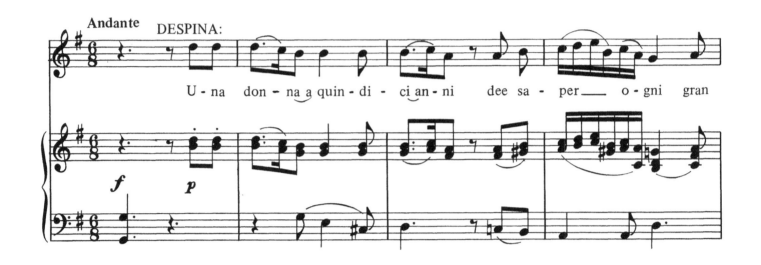

U-na don-na a quin-di-ci an-ni dee sa-per___ o-gni gran

mo-da, do-ve il dia-vo-lo ha la co-da, co-sa è be-ne, e mal cos'

è, dee sa-per___ le ma-li-ziet-te, che in-na—

mo - ra - no gli a - man - ti, fin - ger ri - so, fin - ger pian - ti, in - ven -

tar — i bei per - chè,— fin - ger ri - so, fin - ger pian - ti, in - ven -

Allegretto

tar — i bei per - chè.   Dee in un mo -

men — to dar ret - ta a cen - to, col - le pu - pil - le par - lar con mil - le,

p

gi - na col «pos - so e vo - glio» far - si ub - bi - dir.

f *p*

Par ch'ab-bian gu - sto di tal dot - tri - na; vi - va De -

spi - na, che sa ser - vir,_____ che sa ser - vir.

Dee in un mo - men - to dar ret - ta a a cen - to, col - le pu

pil - le par - lar con mil - le,

dar spe - me a tut - ti, sien bel - li o brut - ti, sa - per_ na -

scon - der-si, sen - za_ con - fon - der-si, sen za ar-ros - si - re, sa - per men -

ti - re, sa-per men - ti - re. E qual re - gi - na dall' al - to so glio col «pos - so e

f p   *f p*   *f p*

dir,＿ sì,＿ far - si ub - bi - dir.

Par ch'ab-bian gu — sto di tal dot—tri — na; vi - va De—

spi — na, che sa ser - vir, vi - va De - spi - na, che sa ser - vir, vi - va De—

spi — na, che sa ser - vir,＿ che sa ser - vir,＿ che sa ser - vir.

S'altro che lagrime

from
LA CLEMENZA DI TITO

non gio - ve - rà. A_ quest' in - u - ti-le pie - ta _____ che

sen - ti, o_ quan - to è si - mi-le la cru - del - tà, La_

cru - del - tà. S'al - tro che la - gri-me per_ lui non_

ten - ti, tut - to il tuo pian - ge-re _____ non gio - ve -

rà,_____ tut - to il tu - o pian-ge-re, tut to il tu - o

pian-ge-re non gio - ve - rà,_____ non gio - ve -

rà,_____ non gio - ve - rà.

Ach, ich fühl's

from
DIE ZAUBERFLÖTE

Andante

PAMINA:

Ach, ich fühls, es ist ver-schwun-den, e - wig hin der Lie - be Glück, e - wig hin der Lie - be Glück! Nim - mer kommt ihr, Won - ne-stun-den, mei - nem Her - zen mehr zu-rück, mei - nem Her - zen, mei - nem

sein. Fühlst du nicht der Lie-be Seh - nen, fühlst du— nicht der Lie - be

cresc. _f_ _p_

Sehnen, so——wird Ru - he,— so——wird Ruh im—To - de— sein, so wird

Ruh——— im To - de sein, im To - de sein, im To - de—

sein.

_p_ cresc. _f_ _p_